True Taste of Thai

By : **Krongtong Na-Songkhla**

The owner of True Taste of Thai : Thai Home-Cooking Cooked in Your Home!

www.truetasteofthai.com

Designed by : Umaporn Busabok

Copyright ©2012 by : Krongtong Na-Songkhla
All rights reserved.

Contents

Stir Fry

Noodles

Dessert & Beverages

Rice & Sticky Rice

Introduction

Do you enjoy eating Thai cuisine but feel intimidated by its countless curries and seemingly exotic ingredients?

Have you never set foot in an Asian grocery store because you know you'd feel completely lost?

Does your Thai cookbook include recipes with catchy names but full of substitute ingredients?

Would you like to learn how to cook delicious, authentic Thai dishes at home using the proper ingredients?

With today's lifestyle and tight economy, more people are choosing to dine at home. My goal is to provide budget-friendly dishes with amazing authentic Thai flavor while at the same time improving your comfort level with the many unique ingredients used throughout Thai cuisine. Venturing into the unknown brings anxiety and doubt, but you can master the preparation of these simple, home-cooked meals right in your own home!

Often times, people have asked me to recommend a good Thai restaurant. I always answer back "At Your Own Home!" I haven't gone out for Thai food for years after repeatedly being disappointed with the lack of authenticity of some restaurants.

I've prepared these recipes based on my childhood memories, family recipes, and teaching experiences. They are quick to cook and simple to follow recipes using many ingredients you can now find at your local supermarket. And with the growing popularity of Asian grocers, you can dive even deeper into the True Taste of Thai food if you dare!

A special thank you too all my students for encouraging me to put together my own cook book. We have shared new culinary experiences together using readily available ingredients and with surprisingly little effort. Thanks also to my family for their help and encouragement. I hope everyone can now enjoy making these True Taste of Thai dishes in the comfort of your own home!

About the author

Krongtong Na-Songkhla (known as Krong), a Thai native, first learned Thai cooking as a child in the southern province of Songkhla, Thailand. She spent many years helping her mother and grandmother prepare everyday meals for her family.

While studying for her MBA at the University of Michigan, Krong missed the unique flavors of Thailand which she so loved. Unable to find necessary ingredients for her own recipes, she worked to develop techniques and to modify recipes yet keep the **True Taste of Thai** in all her dishes.

Since 2001, Krong has lived in New York, Texas, Michigan, and Indiana, and traveled around the country. Along her path, many of Krong's family and friends have inquired about Thai cooking. Now settled in San Diego area with her husband, Krong developed **True Taste of Thai** (www.truetasteofthai.com) in order to share her experience and knowledge with others. She has also been a featured instructor at culinary schools in the area.

Since many people may be intimidated by seemingly exotic ingredients, it is Krong's goal to ease your worries and encourage you to experience the amazing world of Thai cuisine!

Sauces

Sesame Oil

Black Sweet Soy Sauce

Chili Oil

Fish Sauce

Light Soy Sauce

Plum Sauce

Oyster Sauce

Nam Prik Pao (roasted chili paste)

Mirin (Japanese cooking wine)

Rice Vinegar

Seasoning Sauce

Soy Bean Paste

Sweet Chili Sauce

Curry Paste

Green Curry Paste   Massaman Curry Paste   Panang Curry Paste   Red Curry Paste   Yellow Curry Paste

Canned

Coconut Milk   Shredded Bamboo Shoots   Water Chestnut

Flour

Tao Yai Mom (Arrow Root Flour)

Glutinous Rice Flour

Rice Flour

Tapioca Flour

Corn Flour

Noodles

Egg (Yellow) Noodles

Glass Noodles
(Mung Bean Vermicelli)

Fresh Wide Rice Noodles

Rice Stick Noodles (Dried)

Dry Spices

Deep Fried Shallot

Cardamom Seeds

Dried Thai Chili Powder

Roasted Rice Powder

Chinese Five-Spice Powder

Curry Powder

Deep Fried Garlic

White Sesame Seeds

Turmeric

Whole Dried Chili Peppers (small)

White Pepper Powder

Whole Dried Chili Peppers (big)

Vegetables & Fruits

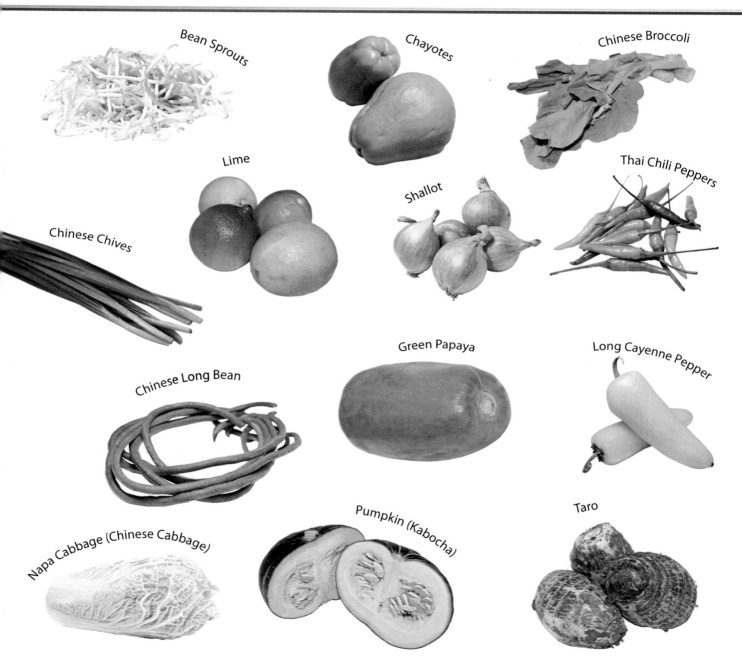

Bean Sprouts

Chayotes

Chinese Broccoli

Lime

Shallot

Thai Chili Peppers

Chinese Chives

Green Papaya

Long Cayenne Pepper

Chinese Long Bean

Taro

Napa Cabbage (Chinese Cabbage)

Pumpkin (Kabocha)

Herbs

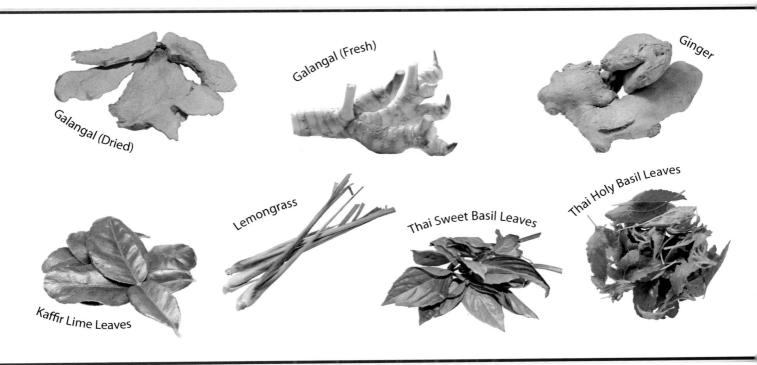

Galangal (Dried)

Galangal (Fresh)

Ginger

Kaffir Lime Leaves

Lemongrass

Thai Sweet Basil Leaves

Thai Holy Basil Leaves

Wrappers

Spring Roll Wrappers

SPRING ROLL SHELLS

Won Ton Skins

Wonton Wrappers

Tofu

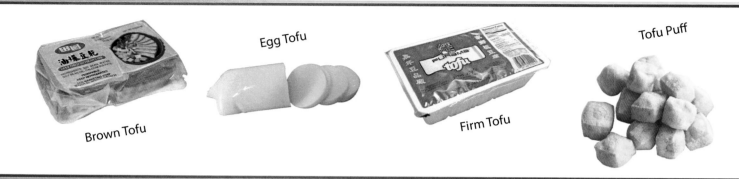

Brown Tofu

Egg Tofu

Firm Tofu

Tofu Puff

Useful Utensils

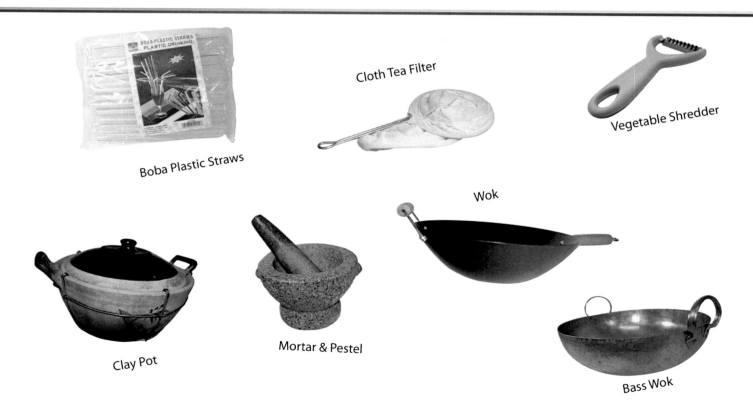

Boba Plastic Straws

Cloth Tea Filter

Vegetable Shredder

Clay Pot

Mortar & Pestel

Wok

Bass Wok

Other

Black Fungus

Boba Tapioca Pearls

Dried Shiitake Mushroom

Chinese Sausage

Dried Pork Fluff

Pickled Mustard

Jasmine Essence

Palm Sugar

Dried Shrimp

Pandan Essence

Preserved Radish

Tamarind Concentrate

Tapioca Pearls (small)

Thai Iced tea Powder

Thai Pork Loaf

Thai Rice Cracker

Appetizers & Snacks

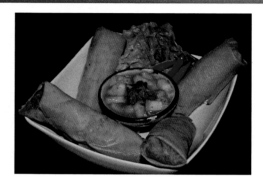

Ingredients:

5 dried Shiitake mushrooms (if available)
1 cup glass noodles (Mung Bean Vermicelli)
1 teaspoon chopped cilantro root (or stem)
1 teaspoon chopped garlic
1 teaspoon white pepper powder
1 tablespoon vegetable oil
1 cup ground pork
1/4 cup thinly shredded carrot
 (or carrot sticks)
2 tablespoons all purpose flour
1 tablespoon water
16 sheets of spring roll wrappers,
 size 4"x4" or bigger
Vegetable oil for deep frying
1/3 cup sweet chili sauce for dipping
1 cucumber, peeled and coarsely diced
Thai basil, mint and lettuce (optional)

Seasoning sauce:

1 tablespoon fish sauce
1 tablespoon sugar
1 tablespoon light soy sauce

Directions: Spring rolls

1. In a small bowl, combine seasoning sauce ingredients and set aside.
2. In a second small bowl, soak dried Shiitake mushrooms in warm water until soft and puffy. Discard hard stems. Finely chop into small pieces.
3. In a third bowl, soak glass noodles in warm water for 15 minutes; then use scissors to cut them into 1" lengths. Set them aside, still in the water; drain when ready to use.
4. Using a mortar and pestle, crush cilantro, garlic, and white pepper powder.
5. Heat 1 tablespoon of vegetable oil in a pan at medium heat. Add cilantro/garlic mixture and stir fry until fragrant.
6. Add pork, drained noodles, shredded carrots, and finely chopped Shiitake mushroom.
7. Stir in seasoning sauce. When pork is half cooked, turn the heat off. The seasoning sauce will have reduced and thickened some. Let meat mixture cool.
8. In a small bowl, mix together water and flour to make a "glue" for sealing the wrappers.
9. Place one spring roll wrapper flat, at an angle to you so that it looks like a diamond shape. It should be soft enough to roll and not break apart. If it is too dry, spray it with water or use a damp cloth to add moisture before adding the filling.
10. In the lower center of the wrapper, place some cooled pork mixture. Tightly fold the bottom edge up to cover the filling. Then fold the left and the right sides toward each other to tightly enclose the meat filling. Lastly, roll the wrapper up to the top. Seal the edge well with the flour and water mixture.
11. Be sure to fold it very tight since it will loosen when you fry it. Set it on a plate and cover with a damp paper towel while you prepare the other spring rolls.
12. Heat oil in a pan at medium heat for deep frying. Add 5 spring rolls each time and keep turning them until brown and crispy all over.
13. Remove from pan and place them on paper to remove excess oil.
14. In a small bowl, combine sweet chili sauce and coarsely diced cucumber to make a dipping sauce.
15. Serve spring rolls on a platter with the dipping sauce and fresh vegetables such as Thai basil, mint, and lettuce.

Tod Man Kao Pod - Deep Fried Pork Cake with Corn

Ingredients:

1/2 cup corn, fresh or canned
1 teaspoon chopped cilantro root (or stem)
1 teaspoon chopped garlic
1 teaspoon white pepper powder
1/4 cup ground pork
1 egg yolk
1/4 cup all purpose flour
1 teaspoon salt
1 teaspoon sugar
Vegetable oil for deep frying
1/3 cup sweet chili sauce for dipping
1 cucumber, peeled and coarsely diced
Thai basil, mint and lettuce (optional)

Directions:

1. Using a mortar and pestle, slightly pound corn and set it aside.
2. Using a mortar and pestle, crush cilantro root (or stem), chopped garlic, and white pepper powder until fine.
3. In a mixing bowl, combine ground pork, corn, cilantro/garlic mixture, egg yolk, all purpose flour, salt, and sugar. Mix all together well.
4. Form the dough into 1 inch thick balls; flatten slightly.
5. Heat oil in a pan at medium heat for deep frying.
6. Place seasoned pork in oil until golden brown and crispy.
7. Remove from pan and place it on paper to remove excess oil.
8. Serve with sweet chili sauce mixed with coarsely diced cucumber for dipping sauce. Eat with fresh vegetables like Thai basil, mint, and lettuce.

Khanom Pang Na Kung - Thai Style Shrimp Toasts

Ingredients:

8 slices white sandwich bread, dried
1/2 lb raw shrimp, shelled and deveined
1 tablespoon cilantro, finely chopped
1 large garlic clove, finely chopped
1 egg white
1 tablespoon white sesame seeds
Vegetable oil for deep frying
1/3 cup sweet chili sauce for dipping
1 cucumber, peeled and coarsely diced
Thai basil, mint, and lettuce (optional)

Seasoning sauce:

1 teaspoon fish sauce
1/2 teaspoon sugar

Directions:

1. In a small bowl, combine seasoning sauce ingredients and set aside.
2. The bread should not be fresh but dry. You can leave it out to air overnight at room temperature or place it on trays in an oven at 250°F for approximately 30 minutes.
3. Remove crust from dry bread (or keep it if you prefer) and cut each slice into 4 sections.
4. Place shrimp in a food processor and process a few seconds only. If you don't have a food processor, just use a knife to chop up all shrimp on a cutting board.
5. Add chopped cilantro, chopped garlic, egg white, and seasoning sauce ingredients to the food processor (or mixing bowl). Then process again to mix these ingredients about 5 seconds.
6. Spread the shrimp mixture on top of each piece of bread, taking care to reach the edges.
7. Sprinkle white sesame seeds over the shrimp bread.
8. Heat oil in a pan at medium heat for deep frying. Add shrimp toasts in batches. Place the shrimp side down first and fry it until it turns brown. Flip and fry another side as well. Be careful not to burn it. Drain well on paper towels.
9. In a small bowl, combine sweet chili sauce and coarsely diced cucumber to make a dipping sauce.
10. Serve on a platter with the dipping sauce and fresh vegetables such as Thai basil, mint, and lettuce.

Krabueng Talay - Crunchy Spring Roll Sheets with Ground Pork & Shrimp

Ingredients:

1 teaspoon chopped cilantro root (or stem)
1 teaspoon chopped garlic
1 teaspoon white pepper powder
1/4 cup ground pork
1/4 cup ground shrimp
1 tablespoon tapioca flour (or corn starch)
2 tablespoons all purpose flour
1 tablespoon water
4 sheets of spring roll wrappers (8"x8")
Vegetable oil for deep frying
1/3 cup sweet chili sauce for dipping
1 cucumber, peeled and coarsely diced
Thai basil, mint and lettuce (optional)

Seasoning sauce:

1 teaspoon light soy sauce
1 teaspoon sugar
1 teaspoon oyster sauce

Directions: Krabueng Talay

1. In a small bowl, combine seasoning sauce ingredients and set aside.
2. Using a mortar and pestle, crush chopped cilantro root (or stem), garlic, and white pepper powder. Set it aside.
3. In a mixing bowl, combine ground pork, ground shrimp, tapioca flour, cilantro/garlic mixture, and seasoning sauce ingredients. Mix well.
4. In a small bowl, mix together all purpose flour and water to make "glue" for sealing the wrappers.
5. Put one sheet of spring roll wrapper on a flat area. Spread the meat filling on top and smooth it over the sheet.
6. Put another sheet of spring roll wrapper on top of the meat. Press the two sheets together to compact the filling and remove any air spaces. Use the flour glue to seal all edges. Cut it as picture shown below.

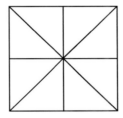

7. Heat oil in a pan at medium-high heat. Deep fry each Krabueng Talay and keep stirring until both sides are browned.
8. Remove from pan and place on paper to remove excess oil.
9. In a small bowl, combine sweet chili sauce and coarsely diced cucumber to make a dipping sauce.
10. Serve on a platter with the dipping sauce and fresh vegetables such as Thai basil, mint, and lettuce.

Ingredients:

1/2 lb tilapia fillet - cut into chunks
(or any kind of white fish)
1 egg
1 1/2 teaspoon red curry paste
3 Kaffir lime leaves, halved and finely sliced
1 tablespoon fish sauce
1 tablespoon chopped cilantro
1 tablespoon corn flour
1/4 cup fresh green beans, thinly sliced
Vegetable oil for shallow frying
1/3 cup sweet chili sauce for dipping
1 cucumber, peeled and coarsely diced
Thai basil, mint, and lettuce (optional)

Directions:

1. Place fish, egg, and red curry paste into a food processor and use the pulse button to combine all of the ingredients.
2. Place into a bowl and mix in finely sliced Kaffir lime leaves, fish sauce, chopped cilantro, corn flour, and sliced green beans.
3. Dip your fingers into cold water and form fish mixture (a tablespoon at a time) into rounds the size of golf balls, flatten to form round patties.
4. Heat oil in a flat pan and place fish cakes into the pan, turning over after about 2 minutes.
5. In a small bowl, combine sweet chili sauce and coarsely diced cucumber to make a dipping sauce.
6. Serve on a platter with the dipping sauce and fresh vegetables such as Thai basil, mint, and lettuce.

Kao Tang Na Tang - Pork and Shrimp in Coconut Sauce for Rice Crackers

Ingredients:
3/4 cup roasted peanuts
1/4 lb shrimp, peeled and deveined
1 can (13.5 oz) coconut milk,
    divided 1/2 cup + 1/4 cup
3/4 lb ground pork
1 shallot, thinly sliced
2 fresh Thai chili peppers, thinly sliced
1 teaspoon chopped cilantro
1 package Thai rice crackers
Cilantro leaves (optional)
Thai chili peppers (optional),
    thinly sliced lengthwise

Seasoning sauce:
1/2 teaspoon salt
2 tablespoons fish sauce
4 tablespoons palm sugar

Ingredients: chili paste
4 garlic cloves
8 dried chili peppers (small)
1/2 teaspoon whole peppercorns

Directions:
1. In a small bowl, combine seasoning sauce ingredients and set aside.
2. In a mortar, combine chili paste ingredients. Using a pestle, crush and blend well until it's smooth and very fine. Set aside.
3. In a food processor or mortar, finely crush peanuts and set aside.
4. On a cutting board, finely dice the shrimp.
5. In a pot, on medium heat, bring to boil about 1/2 cup coconut milk. Then add the chili paste from #2 and stir until thoroughly mixed.
6. Add pork; continue to stir. When meat begins to cook, stir in an additional 1/4 cup coconut milk. Continue stirring.
7. Add the finely diced shrimp and the remaining coconut milk. Continue stirring over heat until the pork and shrimp are thoroughly cooked.
8. Add seasoning sauce and stir well. Simmer for 10 minutes, stirring frequently.
9. Add crushed peanut, sliced shallot, sliced chili peppers and chopped cilantro. Stir thoroughly until it boils and then turn off heat. Put in a serving bowl.
10. Deep fry the rice crackers according to the package or until crispy.
11. Serve the warm dipping sauce in a bowl, garnished with cilantro leaves and sliced chili. Place the rice crackers along the side.

Salad

Yum Kai Yang - Spicy Barbecued Chicken Salad

Directions:

1. In a small bowl, combine seasoning sauce ingredients and set aside.
2. Combine chicken, cilantro, tomato, and onion in a mixing bowl.
3. For best fresh taste, add seasoning sauce in the mixing bowl just before serving. Toss to mix well.
4. Serve on a platter of arranged lettuce leaves and sliced cucumber.

Ingredients:

1 cup shredded rotisserie chicken
1 tablespoon chopped cilantro
2 tomatoes, seeded and cut into chunks
1/4 medium onion, thinly sliced
Lettuce leaves (optional)
Cucumber, peeled and sliced (optional)

Seasoning sauce:

2 tablespoons lime juice
1 tablespoon + 1 1/2 teaspoon fish sauce
1 teaspoon sugar
1 tablespoon Nam Prik Pao
   (roasted chili paste)
1/4 teaspoon dried Thai chili powder

Yum Moo Yok - Spicy Thai Pork Loaf Salad

Ingredients:
1/2 Thai pork loaf
4 cups water
1/4 medium onion, thinly sliced
2 tomatoes, seeded and cut into chunks
1 green onion, coarsely chopped
Lettuce leaves (optional)

Seasoning sauce:
1 tablespoon lime juice
1 tablespoon + 1 teaspoon fish sauce
1 1/2 teaspoon sugar
1/4 teaspoon dried Thai chili powder
3 fresh Thai chili peppers,
    thin slices crosswise

Directions:
1. In a small bowl, combine seasoning sauce ingredients and set aside.
2. Divide the pork loaf into quarter sections. (Cut in half lengthwise; cut each one again lengthwise.) Cut again into 1/4" thick slices.
3. Bring water to boil in a pot on high heat.
   Add pork slices and boil about 2 minutes. Drain.
4. For best fresh taste, combine cooked pork loaf, all vegetables, and the seasoning sauce. in the mixing bowl just before serving. Toss to mix well.
5. Spoon the salad onto a bed of green lettuce leaves arranged on a plate and serve immediately.

Ingredients:

1 cup glass noodles (Mung Bean Vermicelli)
1/4 cup ground chicken or pork
1/4 cup water
A pinch of salt
1/4 cup shredded carrot (or carrot stick)
1/4 cup thinly sliced white onion
2 Roma tomatoes, seeded and sliced thin
1 tablespoon cilantro leaves
2 tablespoons roasted peanuts
Lettuce leaves (optional)

Seasoning sauce:

2 tablespoons fish sauce
2 teaspoons sugar
2 tablespoons lime juice
3 fresh Thai chili peppers,
    thin slices crosswise
1/4 teaspoon dried Thai chili powder

Directions:

1. In a small bowl, combine seasoning sauce ingredients and set aside.
2. Soak glass noodles in warm water about 30 minutes to partially soften. Then cut into 2" lengths. Set them aside, still in the water; drain when ready to use.
3. In a small pot, completely cook ground chicken (or pork) with the 1/4 cup water and salt.
4. Add drained noodles to the cooked chicken and continue mixing well over heat until glass noodles turn soft, clear and transparent. Remove from heat.
5. Transfer noodles and chicken (or pork) to a mixing bowl. Add carrot, white onion, and tomato.
6. For best fresh taste, add seasoning sauce in the mixing bowl just before serving. Toss to mix well.
7. Serve on a platter of arranged lettuce leaves. Garnish with cilantro leaves and roasted peanuts.

Phla Kung - Sliced Shrimp Salad

Directions:

1. In a small bowl, combine seasoning sauce ingredients. Mix well together and set aside.
2. In a medium pot, bring water to a boil. Add shrimp and cook thoroughly. Drain and set shrimp aside.
3. For best fresh taste, mix shrimp, vegetables, and seasoning sauce in the mixing bowl just before serving. Toss to mix well.
4. Place lettuce leaves on a plate and top with the shrimp salad.

Ingredients:

1/2 lb shrimp, peeled and deveined
2 Thai chili peppers, thin slices crosswise
1 stalk lemongrass, thin slices crosswise
3 shallots, thinly sliced
20 mint leaves
1 tablespoon kaffir lime leaf, halved and
   finely sliced
Lettuce leaves (optional)

Seasoning sauce:

1/4 teaspoon sugar
1 tablespoon lime juice
1 tablespoon fish sauce
1 tablespoon Nam Prik Pao
   (roasted chili paste)

Ingredients:
1 lb steak, 1 – 1 1/2" thick

Ingredients: for beef marinade
3 tablespoons fish sauce
3 tablespoons black sweet soy sauce

Directions: Beef
1. Combine marinade ingredients. Add meat and let sit for at least 30 minutes.
2. Barbeque, broil or grill steak on the rare side of medium-rare.
3. Cut into bite-sized pieces and refrigerate till ready to use.

Remaining ingredients:
1/4 cup water
4 tablespoons fish sauce
4 tablespoons lime juice
2 tablespoons shallots, thinly sliced
2 tablespoons chopped cilantro
10 mint leaves
2 tablespoons roasted rice powder*
1/4 teaspoon dried Thai chili powder

Directions:
1. In a pan, bring 1/4 cup of water to boil on medium high heat and add the strips of grilled beef, immediately followed by all the remaining ingredients.
2. Stir until heated through (about a minute). The meat should cook to medium-rare. Turn off the heat.
3. Serve with Thai sticky rice or as part of a meal.

Directions: Roasted rice powder*
1. In a medium-sized pan, over fairly hot heat, constantly stir a couple table spoons of uncooked jasmine rice until it turns golden brown.
2. Remove from heat. When cooled, use a mortar and pestle, a food processor, or a pepper mill to grind rice to a fairly coarse texture. Keep it in a jar.

Grilled

Kai Yang - Grilled, Marinated Chicken Served with Spicy & Sour Dipping Sauces

Ingredients: Chicken
4 pieces of chicken thighs (or any part of chicken you prefer)
1 teaspoon chopped cilantro stems
1 teaspoon chopped garlic
1 teaspoon white pepper powder
4 tablespoons coconut milk
2 teaspoons whiskey (optional)
1/4 cup coconut milk (for basting)

Seasoning sauce: marinade chicken
1 tablespoon light soy sauce
1 tablespoon seasoning soy sauce
1 tablespoon oyster sauce

Directions: Chicken
1. Remove bones from chicken thighs. Pierce meat with a fork and place in a mixing bowl.
2. Crush cilantro, garlic, and white pepper powder in a mortar well. Add to the bowl of chicken.
3. Add coconut milk, whiskey, and seasoning sauce ingredients. Mix well and marinate chicken at least 30 minutes or overnight for a better flavor.
4. Barbeque the chicken over charcoal or broil until cooked through and the skin is crispy brown. If grilling, brush both sides of the chicken with coconut milk for basting. Flip chicken only once to keep it crispy.

5. Serve chicken, cut into bite-sized pieces, along with sticky rice and spicy & sour sauce or sweet chili sauce.

Ingredients: Dipping sauce (spicy & sour sauce)
2 tablespoons fish sauce
2 teaspoons lime juice
2 teaspoons tamarind concentrate
1/4 teaspoon palm sugar
1 teaspoon chopped cilantro
1 teaspoon roasted rice powder* (optional)
1/4 teaspoon dried Thai chili powder

Directions: Dipping sauce
1. Combine the first 4 ingredients and stir until sugar is dissolved.
2. For best fresh taste, add last 3 ingredients just before serving.

Directions: Roasted rice powder*
1. In a medium-sized pan, over fairly hot heat, constantly stir a couple tablespoons of uncooked jasmine rice until it turns golden brown.
2. Remove from heat. When cooled, use a mortar and pestle, a food processor, or a pepper mill to grind rice to a fairly coarse texture. Keep it in a jar.

Kai Satay - Grilled Chicken Skewers Served with Mildly Spicy Peanut Sauce

I. Ingredients: Satay
1 lb chicken breast (or pork tenderloin)
2 tablespoons coconut milk, for basting
A pinch of salt and sugar
2 slices toasted sandwich bread

I. Seasoning sauce: Satay
1/2 tablespoon curry powder
1/4 teaspoon baking soda
1/2 teaspoon turmeric powder
1/2 teaspoon salt
1 1/2 teaspoon sugar
1 tablespoon vegetable oil
1/4 cup coconut milk

I. Directions: satay
1. Soak skewers in water for at least 30 minutes to prevent them from burning when grilled.
2. Cut chicken breast (or pork) into strips 1/4" thick, 1/2" wide, 1" long.
3. Mix well all Satay seasoning sauce ingredients. Add sliced chicken (or pork) and coat well.
4. Marinate in the refrigerator 1 hour or more to enhance flavor of the meat.
5. In a small bowl, combine 2 tablespoons of coconut milk with a little bit of salt and sugar for basting
6. Thread marinated chicken onto skewers. Grill 5 minutes per side, or until cooked through, constantly basting them with the seasoned coconut milk.
7. Serve chicken skewers with side bowls of peanut sauce, cucumber relish and sliced toast.

II. Ingredients: peanut sauce
2 tablespoons vegetable oil
2 tablespoons Massaman curry paste
1 cup coconut milk
1 tablespoon coconut milk + water to make 1/2 cup measure
1/4 cup roasted peanuts, finely chopped

II. Seasoning sauce: peanut sauce
1 tablespoon fish sauce
2 tablespoons palm sugar
1 tablespoon tamarind concentrate

II. Directions: peanut sauce
1. In a small bowl, combine peanut seasoning sauce ingredients and set aside.
2. In a sauce pan, heat oil and briefly fry the Massaman curry paste until fragrant, being careful not to burn it.
3. Slowly add 1 cup coconut milk 1/3 cup at a time. Between additions, bring to a boil and randomly stir while cooking until a thin film of oil appears on the surface.
4. Add seasoning sauce and stir well.
5. Add the coconut milk diluted with water and finely chopped roasted peanuts. Bring to a boil and turn heat off. If you want the sauce thicker, let it simmer for 10-15 minutes more.
6. Pour in a serving bowl as a dipping sauce for Satay.

III. Ingredients: cucumber relish
1/3 cup vinegar	2 shallots, thinly sliced
1/2 cup sugar	2 Thai chili peppers, thinly crosswise
1 teaspoon salt	1 cucumber, very coarsely chopped, or sliced

III. Directions: cucumber relish
1. In a sauce pan, combine vinegar, sugar, and salt and bring to a boil for 2 minutes. Let it cool.
2. In a serving bowl, prepare shallot, chili peppers, and cucumber. For best fresh taste, add the vinegar mixture when ready to serve.

Moo Yang Takrai - Thai Barbequed Pork with Lemongrass

Ingredients:

1 lb pork tenderloin

Ingredients: for pork marinade and dipping sauce

3 tablespoons coconut milk

4 tablespoons palm sugar

4 tablespoons fish sauce

4 tablespoons black sweet soy sauce

4 tablespoons fresh lemongrass,
    finely sliced

2 tablespoons whiskey (optional)

3 tablespoons shallots, thinly sliced

3 tablespoons minced garlic

2 tablespoons sesame oil

1 teaspoon white pepper powder

Directions:

1. Soak skewers in water for at least 30 minutes to prevent them from burning when grilled.
2. Cut pork into strips 1/4" thick, 2" wide, 2" long and set aside.
3. Set coconut milk aside. Then mix all other ingredients in a saucepan.
4. Simmer until volume is reduced by about one half. Allow to cool.
5. Stir in coconut milk. Mix in the pork and coat well.
6. Marinade for 1-3 hours. Then remove the pork and set aside all marinade in a pot.
7. Thread marinated pork onto skewers and grill till cooked through.
8. Bring reserved marinade to boil for 5 minutes. Turn the heat down and simmer for 10 minutes to make a dipping sauce.
9. Serve on a platter with dipping sauce # 8 in a separate bowl on the side.

Soup & Curry

Ingredients:

2 tablespoons vegetable oil

2 tablespoons green curry paste

1 cup coconut milk

2 chicken breasts,
   cut into small bite-sized pieces

2 tablespoons coconut milk + water to make
   1 cup measure

1/2 cup canned bamboo shoot (optional)

2 kaffir lime leaves, tear in half and remove
   central stem

3 Thai chili peppers for garnish,
   long thin slices

1/4 cup Thai sweet basil leaves

Seasoning sauce:

3 tablespoons fish sauce

2 tablespoons palm sugar

Directions:

1. In a small bowl, combine seasoning sauce ingredients and set aside.
2. In a pot, heat the oil and briefly fry the curry paste until fragrant, being careful not to burn it.
3. Slowly add 1 cup coconut milk 1/3 cup at a time. Between additions, bring to a boil and randomly stir while cooking until a thin film of oil appears on the surface.
4. Add chicken and keep on medium heat until chicken is half-cooked. Add seasoning sauce and stir it well.
5. Add the coconut milk diluted with water and the bamboo shoot. Bring to a boil.
6. When chicken is fully cooked, add kaffir lime leaves, chili peppers, and Thai sweet basil leaves. Turn off the heat.
7. Serve with freshly-steamed Thai jasmine rice.

Tom Yum Kung-Thailand's Signature Spicy and Sour Lemongrass Soup and Shrimp

Directions:

1. In a small bowl, combine seasoning sauce ingredients and set aside.
2. Bring chicken broth to a boil. Add lemongrass and sliced galangal.
3. Bring back to a boil and then add mushrooms.
4. Add shrimp. As soon as the shrimp turn pink (cooked through), add seasoning sauce, fresh chili peppers, and kaffir leaves. Turn off the heat.
5. Add coconut milk (or milk) and serve garnished with cilantro.

Ingredients:

1 1/2 cups chicken broth
1 stalk fresh lemongrass, lightly pounded, cut into 2" lengths
1 inch long galangal, sliced thinly (or 3 pieces of dried galangal)
1 cup mushroom, sliced
15 shrimp, peeled and deveined
3 fresh Thai chili peppers, crushed
3 kaffir lime leaves, tear in half and remove central stem
1/4 cup coconut milk (or milk)
Cilantro leaves for garnish

Seasoning sauce:

3 tablespoons fish sauce
2 tablespoons lime juice
1 tablespoon Nam Prik Pao (roasted chili paste)

Ingredients:

1 chicken breast, cut into 1" cubes
1 tablespoon minced fresh ginger root
3 small potatoes
2 tablespoons vegetable oil
2 tablespoons Massaman curry paste
1 cup coconut milk
2 tablespoons coconut milk + water to make
    1 cup measure
3 cardamom seeds (if available)
2 bay leaves
1 cinnamon stick, 2" long
2 tablespoons roasted peanuts

Seasoning sauce:

2 tablespoons fish sauce
2 tablespoons palm sugar
2 tablespoons tamarind concentrate

Directions:

1. In a small bowl, combine seasoning sauce ingredients and set aside.
2. Toss chicken cubes with minced ginger to mix well and let it sit for 15 minutes to enhance flavor and aroma.
3. Peel the potatoes and cut into uniform 2" pieces. Partially cook them in boiling water; drain; set aside.
4. In a pot, heat the oil and briefly fry the Masaman paste until fragrant, being careful not to burn it.
5. Slowly add the 1 cup coconut milk 1/3 cup at a time. Between additions, bring to a boil and randomly stir while cooking until a thin film of oil appears on the surface.
6. Add seasoned chicken and cook on medium heat till chicken is cooked through.
7. Add seasoning sauce and stir well. Add the coconut milk diluted with water and bring to a boil.
8. Add potatoes, cardamom seeds, bay leaves, cinnamon stick, and peanuts. Lower the heat and continue cooking until potatoes are cooked through and the curry (sauce) begins to thicken.
9. Serve with freshly-steamed Thai jasmine rice.

Ingredients:

Warm water, divided (2 cups + 2cups)
1 cup glass noodles (Mung Bean Vermicelli)
5 dried Shiitake mushrooms
1/4 teaspoon black pepper powder
1/4 teaspoon white pepper powder
2 garlic cloves
3/4 cup ground pork
1 1/2 cups chicken broth
1/2 medium white onion, thinly sliced
1/4 head cabbage, coarsely chopped into
    large pieces
2 green onions, cut into 1" pieces
2 teaspoons fried garlic
2 teaspoons chopped cilantro
1/4 teaspoon white pepper powder

Seasoning sauce:

1 tablespoon light soy sauce
1 tablespoon fish sauce

Directions:

1. In a small bowl, combine seasoning sauce ingredients and set aside.
2. In 2 small bowls, with 2 cups warm water each, soak glass noodle, and dried Shiitake mushroom.
3. When mushrooms get plump and soft, remove them from water.
   Slice each mushroom into 4-5 strips and discard its stem.
   Keep the liquid used to soak the mushrooms, this will be used later.
4. In a bowl with glass noodle, after 20 minutes or more, drain water and then use scissors to cut glass noodle a few times into 2"-3" pieces.
5. Using a mortar and pestle, crush black pepper powder, white pepper powder, and garlic into a paste.
6. In a mixing bowl, combine and mix well the garlic paste from # 5, seasoning sauce, and ground pork. Let it sit about 15 minutes to absorb the flavor. Then form into 1" balls.
7. In a pot, bring chicken broth and white onion to a boil.
   Add cabbage and cook until tender.
8. Add pork balls. When the meat begins to cook, add the reserved water from soaking mushrooms.
9. Add cut glass noodles and sliced Shiitake mushrooms. Toss together for a few minutes.
10. Cover and let it boil.
11. Serve in a bowl, topped with green onion, fried garlic, chopped cilantro, and white pepper powder to sprinkle on top of the soup.

Kung Tod Gaeng Ped - Crispy Shrimp with Red Curry

Ingredients:

1 lb raw shrimp, peeled and deveined

2 tablespoons red curry paste

4 tablespoons vegetable oil

2 medium ripe tomatoes, chopped

2 tablespoons lime juice

Directions:

1. Combine shrimp, curry paste and oil in a bowl. Cover with plastic wrap and marinate in the refrigerator for about 30 minutes.

2. Heat a wok or a heavy-based frying pan until it is very hot.
Toss the seasoned shrimp in the curry paste again to coat well.
Then fry the shrimp, in 2-3 batches so as not to overcrowd the wok,
for 3 minutes, tossing frequently.

3. When all shrimp are cooked, remove wok from the heat.
Return all the shrimp to the wok.
Add the tomatoes and lime juice and stir well.

4. Serve immediately with steamed rice.

Chu Chi Kung - Red Curry Shrimp with Kaffir Lime Leaves and Basil

Ingredients:
5 Thai chili peppers
1 cup coconut milk
2 tablespoons red curry paste
1 lb raw shrimp, peeled and deveined
8 kaffir lime leaves, halved and finely sliced
1/2 cup Thai sweet basil leaves

Seasoning sauce:
1 teaspoon fish sauce
2 tablespoons palm sugar

Directions:
1. In a small bowl, combine seasoning sauce ingredients and set aside.
2. Cut 3 Thai chili peppers into thin rounds, including seeds; crush with a mortar and pestle to a coarse paste and set aside. Cut the other 2 peppers with seeds into fine long slivers.
3. Heat 2/3 cup coconut milk in a pan or skillet over medium heat. When it has warmed to a smooth consistency, reserve 1 tablespoon and set aside.
4. Reduce heat to simmer for a few minutes until the coconut milk is thick and bubbly and the oil begins to separate from the milk.
5. Add red curry paste, working it into coconut milk. Stir over medium-high heat for a few minutes, until it is aromatic and darker in color and the mixture is very thick.
6. Increase heat to high and add the remaining 1/3 cup coconut milk, stirring to make a thick, well-blended sauce.
7. Add seasoning sauce and stir well to melt sugar and blend seasonings.
8. Toss shrimp into the sauce and cook, stirring frequently. When most shrimp have lost their raw pink color on the outside, stir in the crushed chili peppers from # 2 and kaffir lime leaves.
9. Stir fry 10 to 15 seconds before adding basil and slivered chili peppers. Stir well to wilt basil and, when shrimp are just cooked through, turn off heat.
10. Transfer to a serving dish and drizzle reserved tablespoon of coconut milk over shrimp.

Ingredients:

1/2 lb ground pork
5 cups water, divided
  (2 cups, 1 cup, and 2 cups)
2 cups chicken broth
4 cups cooked jasmine rice
1 tablespoon light soy sauce
1 green onion, thinly sliced
1 teaspoon chopped cilantro
1/2 small ginger root, thin strips
1/4 teaspoon white pepper powder

Seasoning sauce: for pork

2 tablespoons oyster sauce
1 tablespoon light soy sauce
1 tablespoon seasoning soy sauce
2 teaspoons sugar
1 teaspoon white pepper powder

Directions:

1. Mix ground pork with seasoning sauce thoroughly and set aside.
2. Combine 2 cups water and 2 cups chicken broth in a large pot; bring to boil on medium-high heat.
3. Put cooked rice in food processor; add 1 cup water and blend well. Add rice to the pot. Stir well.
4. Reduce heat to low heat. Simmer for 15 minutes, stirring frequently and remove from heat.
5. In a smaller pot, bring 2 cups water to a boil on medium-high heat. Form pork mixture (a tablespoon at a time) into rounds. Add all pork balls to the boiled water and cook thoroughly; then add 1 tablespoon light soy sauce.
6. Add pork balls and all their liquid to the rice soup pot. Stir well and then remove from heat.
7. Serve immediately in individual bowls. Garnish each with the green onion, cilantro, ginger, and white pepper powder.

Moo Tui - Pork Rib Stewed with Shiitake Mushroom

Ingredients:

5 dried Shiitake mushrooms
4 cups water, divided (2 cups + 2 cups)
1 lb pork spare ribs, cut into 2" lengths
4 garlic cloves
1 teaspoon whole peppercorns
1/2 teaspoon coriander seeds
1 tablespoon sugar
1 teaspoon chopped cilantro
1/4 teaspoon white pepper powder

Seasoning sauce:

1 tablespoon light soy sauce
2 tablespoons seasoning soy sauce
2 tablespoons oyster sauce

Directions:

1. In a small bowl, combine seasoning sauce ingredients and set aside.
2. Soak dried Shiitake mushrooms in 2 cups water.
   When they are soft, press out all the water, cut stems and slice.
   Reserve all the water used here.
3. Bring 2 cups water to a boil in a pot. Add rinsed spare ribs and reduce heat to medium.
4. Thoroughly crush garlic, peppercorns, and coriander seeds in a mortar. Add to the pot.
5. Add seasoning sauce; reduce heat to low and simmer for 1 hour. If you have a pressure cooker, cook for about 30 minutes.
6. Remove the cooked ribs with a spoon and place them into a slow cooker. Cover ribs with sliced Shiitake mushrooms.
7. Strain the water used to cook the ribs and add it to the slow cooker. Also add enough reserved mushroom water to completely cover the ribs and mushrooms.
8. Add sugar and simmer on low heat for 1 hour or until the ribs are tender.
9. Serve pork ribs and stewed mushrooms immediately on a plate. Garnish with chopped cilantro leaves and sprinkle with white pepper powder.

Ingredients:

2 chayotes

2 tablespoons vegetable oil

2 tablespoons red curry paste

1 cup coconut milk

1/2 lb pork tenderloin, cut into small
  bite-sized pieces

2 tablespoons coconut milk + water to make
  1 cup measure

1/4 cup Thai sweet basil leaves

5 kaffir lime leaves, tear in half and remove
  central stem

2 Thai chili peppers, thinly sliced

Seasoning sauce:

3 tablespoons fish sauce

2 tablespoons palm sugar

Directions:

1. In a small bowl, combine seasoning sauce ingredients and set aside.
2. Cut chayote into quarters; remove seeds; peel and wash.
   Then cut into pieces and set aside.
3. In a pot, heat the oil and briefly fry the curry paste until fragrant,
   being careful not to burn it.
4. Slowly add 1 cup coconut milk 1/3 cup at a time. Between additions,
   bring to a boil and randomly stir while cooking until a thin film of oil
   appears on the surface.
5. Add pork pieces and cook on medium heat till cooked through.
   Add seasoning sauce and stir well.
6. Add chayote and the coconut milk diluted with water, stirring thoroughly.
7. Simmer on low heat for 30 minutes.
8. Add the Thai sweet basil leaves, kaffir lime leaves and sliced chili peppers.
   Stir quickly and remove from heat.
9. Spoon pork red curry into a bowl and serve immediately.

Stir Fry

Ingredients:

3 Thai chili peppers

1 tablespoon minced garlic

2 tablespoons vegetable oil

2 chicken breasts,
   cut into small bite-sized pieces

1/4 cup chicken broth

1/4 cup white onion, thinly sliced

1/4 cup Thai holy basil leaves

1/4 teaspoon dried Thai chili powder
   (optional)

Seasoning sauce:

1 tablespoon fish sauce

1 teaspoon sugar

1 tablespoon oyster sauce

1 teaspoon seasoning soy sauce

1 teaspoon black sweet soy sauce

Directions:

1. In a small bowl, combine seasoning sauce ingredients and set aside.
2. Roughly pound chili peppers and garlic together.
3. Heat oil in a wok over medium-high heat and add peppers and garlic mixture. Stir until the aroma rises from the wok and garlic turns golden brown.
4. Add chicken and cook thoroughly.
5. Add seasoning sauce and chicken broth.
6. Add white onion and Thai holy basil leaves. If you prefer it spicier, add dried Thai chili powder to taste.
7. Stir well and turn heat off.
8. Serve on a platter.

Pad Preaw Wahn Kung - Stir Fried Sweet and Sour Shrimp with Mixed Vegetables

Ingredients:

2 tablespoons vegetable oil
1 tablespoon minced garlic
10 shrimp, peeled and deveined
1/2 onion, thinly sliced
1/4 cup carrot, sliced
1/4 cup cucumber or zucchini,
   bite-sized pieces
1/4 cup pineapple chunks
1/4 cup tomato, seeded
1/2 green bell pepper, diced
1/2 cup chicken broth
2 tablespoons Tapioca flour* +
   2 tablespoons water
* You can substitute tapioca flour with
corn flour or quick-mixing thickening flour.

Seasoning sauce:

1 tablespoon light soy sauce
1 tablespoon oyster sauce
1 tablespoon fish sauce
2 teaspoons rice vinegar
3 tablespoons ketchup
1 tablespoon sugar

Directions:

1. In a small bowl, combine seasoning sauce ingredients and set aside.
2. In a wok, heat the oil and add garlic until brown and fragrant.
3. Add shrimp and stir until cooked. Remove from the wok and set aside.
4. Add onion, carrot, cucumber or zucchini, pineapple, tomato,
   and bell pepper. Stir until partially cooked.
5. Add seasoning sauce and chicken broth.
6. Mix tapioca flour with water. Add it to the wok,
   stirring quickly until the liquid begins to thicken.
7. When everything is cooked and tender, add cooked shrimp back into the
   wok. Stir well all together.
8. Serve on a platter.

Kai Look Keuy - Deep Fried Hard Boiled Eggs with Tamarind Sauce

Ingredients:

4 eggs

1 cup vegetable oil, for deep frying

3 tablespoons garlic, thinly sliced

3 tablespoons shallot, thinly sliced

2 dried Thai chili peppers (small),
   cut into 1/2" lengths

Cilantro leaves for garnish

Seasoning sauce:

4 tablespoons palm sugar

4 tablespoons tamarind concentrate

3 tablespoons fish sauce

Directions:

1. Cover eggs with 1" – 2" of cold water in a saucepan.
   Slowly bring to a boil; reduce to simmer for 1 minute.
   Remove from heat; cover with a lid; and let sit for 15 minutes.
   Drain off hot water and cool eggs with cold water for 10 minutes before peeling.

2. In a small bowl, combine seasoning sauce ingredients and set aside.

3. Heat oil in a wok, until very hot. Fry eggs until crispy and brown on the outside.

4. With a spoon, remove eggs to drain on paper towels.
   Then cut the eggs in half.

5. In the same wok, fry until browned, drain and set aside the garlic, shallot, and dried chili peppers, respectively.

6. Drain excess oil from the wok, leaving 1 tablespoon.
   Return to heat and add seasoning sauce. As you stir, it will begin to thicken.
   When sauce starts to boil and you see small bubbles, turn heat off.

7. Serve eggs arranged on a plate, each one topped with fried shallot, garlic, and dried chili peppers. Pour seasoning sauce over all and garnish with cilantro.

Kai Pad Cashew Nuts - Stir Fried Chicken with Cashew Nuts

Ingredients:

2 chicken breasts, cut into small bite-sized
    pieces
1/4 cup tapioca flour or all purpose flour
Vegetable oil, divided
    (1 cup and 1 tablespoon)
1/4 cup roasted cashew nuts
1/4 cup whole dried chili peppers, cut into
    1/2" lengths
1/4 cup white onion, thinly sliced
1/4 cup green bell pepper, sliced
3 green onions, cut into 1" lengths

Seasoning sauce:

2 teaspoons seasoning soy sauce
1 tablespoon oyster sauce
1 tablespoon sugar
2 tablespoons Nam Prik Pao
    (roasted chili paste)

Directions:

1. In a small bowl, combine seasoning sauce ingredients and set aside.
2. Toss sliced chicken thoroughly with flour. Set aside.
3. Heat 1 cup oil in a wok over medium-high heat.
4. Deep fry; drain and set aside respectively the cashew nuts,
    dried chili peppers, and chicken. Carefully empty all the oil from the wok.
5. Return wok to heat and add 1 tablespoon oil. Add seasoning sauce and
    stir; it will begin to thicken. When sauce starts to boil and you see small
    bubbles, turn heat off.
6. Add all fried ingredients to the sauce. Quickly mix everything together.
    Add onion, bell pepper, and green onion. Stir well.
7. Serve on a platter.

Ingredients:

2 tablespoons vegetable oil

2 cloves garlic, minced

1 chicken breast, cut into bite-sized pieces

1/2 cup small broccoli florets

1/2 cup diced carrot

1/2 cup sliced red bell pepper

1/4 cup fresh ginger strips

1/2 cup fresh mushroom

1/2 cup diced ham

   (or sliced Chinese sausage)

1/2 teaspoon white pepper powder

2 1/2 cups cooked rice

   (prepared ahead and refrigerated)

1/4 cup green onion, cut into 1" lengths

Seasoning Sauce:

1 1/2 tablespoons fish sauce

1 tablespoon oyster sauce

1 teaspoon sugar

1 tablespoon Mirin

Directions:

1. In a small bowl, combine seasoning sauce ingredients and set aside.
2. In a wok or skillet, heat vegetable oil on medium-high. Add garlic and stir fry until browned.
3. Add chicken and cook completely.
4. Add broccoli, carrot, red bell pepper, ginger, mushroom, and ham. Stir well.
5. Add seasoning sauce to wok, stirring all ingredients and mixing well.
6. Sprinkle white pepper powder over the mixture and stir fry for a minute or two, until the vegetables begin to soften.
7. Add prepared rice and combine well. Add green onion. Turn heat off.
8. Serve in a bowl. If you have a clay baking pot, pre-heat oven to 375F. Warm the pot and then add the fried rice. Cover with its lid and bake for 20 minutes. Crispy edges around the pot will be a nice bonus.

Khao Pad Sopparot - Thai Pineapple Fried Rice

Ingredients:

1/2 cup raisins

2 teaspoons vegetable oil

2 sticks Chinese sausage (optional)

2 tablespoons butter

3 garlic cloves, minced

1/4 medium white onion, diced small

1 chicken breast, cut into bite-sized pieces

1 cup diced ham

1/4 cup shredded carrot (or carrot sticks)

1 1/2 cups fresh pineapple,
   cut into bite-sized pieces

3 cups cooked rice
   (prepared ahead and refrigerated)

2 eggs, beaten

3 green onions, thinly sliced

Dried pork fluff (optional)

Seasoning Sauce:

2 tablespoons light soy sauce

3 tablespoons oyster sauce

1 tablespoon seasoning soy sauce

1 tablespoon sugar

1/2 teaspoon curry powder

Directions:

1. In a small bowl, combine seasoning sauce ingredients and set aside.
2. Soak raisins in water for 30 minutes or more, rinse and set side.
3. Heat vegetable oil in a wok on medium heat. When oil is hot, fry Chinese sausages until cooked, and then slice into small pieces. Drain all oil out.
4. Add butter to the same wok. When butter melts, add minced garlic, and diced onion. Stir fry until fragrant and onion is partially cooked.
5. Add chicken and cook well. Add diced ham and stir fry until the ham is cooked.
6. Add shredded carrot and stir fry thoroughly. Add pineapple, raisins, and seasoning sauce. Stir well.
7. Add cooked rice to the wok. Stir it carefully to avoid smashing or breaking the rice. Add sliced Chinese sausages.
8. Push everything to one side of the wok and add beaten egg to the cleared space. Let egg slightly cooked and flip rice on top of it for 15 seconds.
9. Stir well. Add sliced green onion, stirring quickly until all ingredients mix together. Remove from heat.
10. Serve immediately on a plate, with a sprinkling of dried pork fluff.

Optional: Place the finished fried rice inside the carved out half-shell of a pineapple; sprinkle it with some dried pork fluff. Bake in the oven at 325F for about 15 minutes before serving.

Moo Tod Gratiem - Thai Fried Pork with Garlic

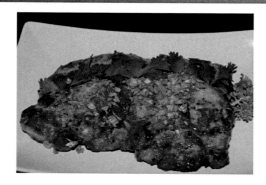

Ingredients:

1/2 lb pork tenderloin, sliced 1/4" thick
1 garlic bulb (about 12 cloves)
1 teaspoon black pepper powder
1 teaspoon white pepper powder
3 tablespoons vegetable oil
Cilantro (garnish)

Seasoning sauce:

2 teaspoons corn starch or all purpose flour
1 tablespoon fish sauce
1 tablespoon soy sauce
1 teaspoon seasoning sauce
1 teaspoon sugar

Directions:

1. In a small bowl, combine seasoning sauce ingredients and set aside.
2. Lightly tenderize the pork with a meat mallet just to break apart the muscle fibers slightly. Then transfer to a mixing bowl.
3. Separate and peel all the cloves of a garlic bulb. Coarsely chop half of them and set aside. Place the remaining half into a mortar and crush them with a pestle. Add black and white pepper powder to crushed garlic and pound again into a garlic paste.
4. Add the garlic paste to the bowl of pork; then add seasoning sauce. Mix well and let it marinate in the refrigerator for 30 minutes or longer.
5. Heat pan and add oil to fry garlic and quickly remove it as soon as it gets brown and drain on a paper towel for a few minutes. Set aside.
6. In the same pan, add marinated pork. Over medium heat (not too high), brown both sides of the pork, being careful not to overcook it. Remove from pan.
7. Serve pork topped with fried garlic and garnished with cilantro.

Ingredients:

Vegetable oil, divided
  (1 teaspoon + 1 tablespoon)

3 eggs, beaten

1/2 cup ground chicken

3 tablespoons diced Roma tomatoes

3 tablespoons mix vegetables
  (fresh or frozen)

2 tablespoons minced onion

1 teaspoon chopped cilantro, for garnish

1 Thai red chili pepper, thinly sliced
  lengthwise

Seasoning sauce:

2 teaspoons sugar

1 1/2 tablespoons fish sauce

1/4 teaspoon black soy sauce

1/4 teaspoon white pepper powder

2 teaspoons ketchup

Directions:

1. In a small bowl, combine seasoning sauce ingredients and set aside.
2. Heat a small non-stick pan 8" in diameter and add 1 teaspoon of oil.
   Add just enough egg to thinly cover the base.
   Brown the omelet lightly on both sides and set it aside.
3. Heat 1 tablespoon of vegetable oil in a wok on medium heat and stir fry
   ground chicken for 2 minutes or until cooked through.
4. Add tomatoes, mixed vegetables, onion, and seasoning sauce.
   Stir fry another 2 to 3 minutes until cooked; then set aside.
5. To stuff the omelet, place the meat mixture in the center.
   Fold two opposite sides toward the center and then fold in the remaining
   sides so that the omelet forms a square.
6. Place omelet on a serving plate and garnish with chopped cilantro and
   thinly sliced red chili. Serve with the jasmine rice.

Directions:

1. In a small bowl, combine seasoning sauce ingredients for step 2 and set aside.
2. Toss chicken with light soy sauce and marinade for 15 minutes or longer.
3. Heat oil in a wok. Add garlic and sauté until golden brown.
4. Add chicken and stir fry briefly over high heat for 5 minutes.
5. Add onion, chili peppers and broccoli. Stir well.
6. Gently add prepared rice to the wok and seasoning sauce. Stir carefully to avoid smashing or breaking the rice.
7. Push everything to one side of the wok and add beaten egg to the cleared space. Let egg slightly cooked and flip rice on top of it for 15 seconds.
8. Thoroughly mix everything. Add tomato and green onion; then stir fry for just a brief minute or two.
9. Remove from heat. Serve garnished with chopped cilantro and white pepper powder.

Ingredients: Step 1

1 chicken breast, cut into bite-sized pieces
2 tablespoons light soy sauce

Ingredients: Step 2

2 tablespoons vegetable oil
1 tablespoon garlic, finely chopped
1/2 medium onion, thinly sliced
3 fresh Thai chili peppers, sliced
1/2 cup broccoli, cut into small florets
3 cups cooked jasmine rice
   (prepared ahead and refrigerated)
2 eggs, lightly beaten, with a pinch of salt
1 tomato, cut into wedges
2 green onions, thinly sliced
2 tablespoons chopped cilantro
1/2 teaspoon white pepper powder

Seasoning sauce: Step 2

1 tablespoon seasoning soy sauce
1 1/2 tablespoons fish sauce
2 tablespoons Nam Prik Pao
   (roasted chili paste)
1 tablespoon lime juice
1 teaspoons sugar

Pad Khana Nam Mun Hoy - Stir fried Chinese Broccoli with Oyster Sauce

Directions:

1. In a small bowl, combine seasoning sauce ingredients and set aside.
2. Discard yellow or hard leaves of the Chinese broccoli and peel stems' skin. Rinse and pat dry. Then cut leaves into 2" lengths and slice the peeled stems.
3. Heat oil in a wok on medium-high heat. When oil is hot, add minced garlic and chili peppers; fry until fragrant.
4. Add Chinese broccoli and seasoning sauce. Stir fry until broccoli is tender. Then remove from heat.
5. Immediately serve on a plate.

Ingredients:

1/2 lb Chinese broccoli (Gai Lan)
2 tablespoons vegetable oil
3 cloves garlic, minced
2 fresh chili peppers, thinly sliced lengthwise

Seasoning sauce:

3 tablespoons oyster sauce
2 tablespoons water

Directions:

1. In a small bowl, combine seasoning sauce ingredients and set aside.
2. Coarsely pound black peppercorns in a mortar.
3. Heat oil in a wok on medium-high heat. When oil is hot, add sliced onion and fry until fragrant.
4. Add sliced pork, black peppercorns and seasoning sauce; stir fry till pork is cooked through.
5. Add long cayenne pepper slices (or bell peppers) and cut green onion. Mix well and remove from heat.
6. Serve immediately on a plate.

Ingredients: Ingredients:

2 tablespoons black peppercorns
1 tablespoon vegetable oil
1/2 medium white onion, thinly sliced
3/4 lb pork tenderloin, thinly sliced 1/8" x 1"
1 fresh long cayenne pepper (or green, red bell peppers), sliced
2 green onions, cut into 1" lengths

Seasoning sauce:

3 tablespoons oyster sauce
1 tablespoon light soy sauce
2 teaspoons sugar

Noodles

Pad Thai - Thin Rice Noodles and Tofu, in Tamarind Based Sauce

Ingredients:

7 oz rice stick noodles
2 tablespoons vegetable oil (divided)
1/4 cup diced firm tofu
12 deveined shrimp (or 1 chicken breast)
1 teaspoon minced garlic
2 teaspoons minced shallot
2 tablespoons chopped sweet radish
   (if available)
2 eggs lightly beaten (divided)
1/2 cup fresh Chinese chives
   (or green onion), cut into 1" lengths

Seasoning sauce:

4 tablespoons fish sauce
3 tablespoons palm sugar
4 tablespoons tamarind concentrate

Ingredients for garnish:

1 cup fresh bean sprouts
Fresh chives, cut into 4" lengths
Slices of lime
Chopped roasted peanuts
Dried Thai chili powder

Directions:

1. Soak the rice stick noodles in warm water for 30 – 45 minutes. Leave in the water until you are ready to use.
2. In a small saucepan, combine all seasoning sauce ingredients. Cook on low heat until the palm sugar dissolves; then increase heat. When it starts to boil, quickly remove from heat and set aside. Pad Thai sauce may be stored in a tightly sealed jar and refrigerated up to a week.
3. Heat 1 tablespoon of oil in a wok at medium-high heat. Add firm tofu and fry until browned and firm. Transfer to a plate and set aside.
4. Add shrimp and cook until done. Set it aside with browned tofu.
5. In the same wok, add another 1 tablespoon of oil. Add garlic and shallot; fry until aromatic. Add radish and stir for 1 minute.
6. Add noodles and stir until soft. If needed, add more water to help the noodles cook until they are soft enough to fall apart easily when pinched with your fingers.
7. Add tofu and seasoning sauce. Stir for about 2-3 minutes. The noodles will absorb the seasoning sauce.
8. Push wok ingredients to one side. In the space created, add one beaten egg and then fold some noodles into it. Push everything to one side again and repeat the process with the second beaten egg. Let everything sit for 15 seconds and then mix together thoroughly.
9. Add Chinese chives and cooked shrimp.
10. Stir well until everything blends together.
11. Turn off heat and transfer to a serving plate. Serve each garnish in a separate dish along the side of the main dish platter.

Pad Woon Sen - Stir Fried Glass Noodle with Egg and Shrimp

Ingredients:

1 1/2 cups glass noodles
(Mung Bean Vermicelli)
3 dried Shiitake mushrooms
2 tablespoons vegetable oil
1/2 medium white onion, thinly sliced
8 shrimp, peeled and deveined
1/3 cup shredded carrot
2 eggs
1 Roma tomato, seeded and cut into wedges
2 green onions, cut into 1" lengths
1 tablespoon, chopped cilantro
1/2 teaspoon white pepper powder

Seasoning sauce:

1 tablespoon light soy sauce
1 teaspoon seasoning soy sauce
2 tablespoons oyster sauce
2 teaspoons sugar

Directions:

1. In a small bowl, soak glass noodles in warm water about 30 minutes. When softened, cut into 2" lengths.
2. In another small bowl, soak dried Shiitake mushrooms in 1/4 cup warm water about 15 minutes. After softening, discard the stems and slice mushrooms into thin pieces. Reserve the water for later use.
3. Combining seasoning sauce ingredients in a small bowl and set aside.
4. Heat oil in a wok at medium-high heat. Add white onion and fry until fragrant and clear.
5. Add shrimp, carrot, and sliced Shiitake mushroom. Add seasoning sauce and stir fry.
6. Add eggs and continue to stir fry quickly, scrambling egg into small pieces.
7. Add glass noodles and the reserved water from soaking the mushrooms.
8. Add tomato and green onion. Stir and blend well.
9. Turn off heat. Transfer to a serving plate and top with cilantro and white pepper powder.

Ingredients:

1 lb pork tenderloin, thinly sliced 1/8"
1/2 lb fresh wide rice noodles
1 lb Chinese broccoli
Sliced carrots and mushrooms (optional)
4 tablespoons vegetable oil, (divided 2 + 2)
2 tablespoons black sweet soy sauce
5 cloves garlic, minced
3 cups water
3 tablespoons tapioca flour* +
    3 tablespoons water
2 tablespoons salted soy bean
1/2 teaspoon white pepper powder
*You can substitute tapioca flour with
corn flour or quick-mixing thickening flour.

Seasoning sauce:

2 tablespoons light soy sauce
1 tablespoon seasoning soy sauce
2 tablespoons oyster sauce
1 tablespoon sugar

Directions:

1. Cut thinly sliced pork into 2" long pieces.
2. In a small bowl, combine seasoning sauce ingredients and set aside.
3. Place wide rice noodles on a plate and cover with plastic wrap. Heat in microwave about 3 minutes. Let it sit for 5 minutes and then separate clumped noodles into single strips.
4. Discard yellow or hard leaves of the Chinese broccoli and peel stems' skin. Cut leaves into 2" lengths and slice peeled stems.
5. Heat 2 tablespoons oil in a wok on medium heat. When oil is hot, add separated noodles and black sweet soy sauce. Stir fry until noodles are completely covered with sauce. Remove from wok; set aside and keep warm.
6. Add 2 more tablespoons oil to the wok on medium heat. Add minced garlic and fry until fragrant.
7. Add sliced pork and stir until partially cooked.
8. Add 3 cups water and bring to a boil. Add seasoning sauce and stir all ingredients until the pork is cooked through. Meanwhile, mix flour with 3 tablespoons water, stirring till well blended; set aside for later use.
9. Add salted soy bean and bring to a boil again.
10. When wok ingredients boil, add broccoli, and any optional vegetables.. Quickly stir in flour thickener so as to avoid clumping. If the sauce is not thick enough, add more flour mixture. The wok liquid will turn from white to clear as it cooks. When sauce bubbles, remove from heat.
11. Transfer noodles to a serving plate. Top with sauce and a sprinkling of white pepper powder. Serve hot.

Kua Kai - Stir Fried Wide Rice Noodles with Chicken

Ingredients: Step 1
2 chicken breasts, cut into small bite-sized
   pieces

Ingredients: Step 1 for marinated chicken
1 tablespoon light soy sauce
2 teaspoons seasoning soy sauce
2 tablespoons oyster sauce
1 teaspoon ground black pepper
2 teaspoons sugar
1 teaspoon sesame oil

Ingredients: Step 2
1/2 lb fresh wide rice noodles
1 tablespoon vegetable oil
3 cloves garlic, minced
2 tablespoons preserved radish, chopped
3 eggs
2 green onions, thinly sliced
4 leaves green lettuce (optional)
1/2 teaspoon white pepper powder

Seasoning sauce: Step 2
2 tablespoons light soy sauce
2 tablespoons seasoning soy sauce
1 tablespoon sugar

Directions:
1. In a mixing bowl, combine marinade ingredients thoroughly.
   Add cut chicken and coat well. Let sit for a minimum of 30 minutes or more.
2. Place wide rice noodles on a plate and cover with plastic wrap.
   Heat in microwave about 3 minutes. Let it sit for 5 minutes and then
   separate clumped noodles into single strips.
3. In a small bowl, combine seasoning sauce ingredients and set aside.
4. Heat oil in a wok on medium heat. When oil is hot, add minced garlic and
   chopped preserved radish. Fry until fragrant and then add marinated
   chicken.
5. Stir fry until the chicken is nearly cooked. Make a well in the middle;
   add eggs and beat with a spatula.
6. Continue stir frying until eggs are cooked; then push all ingredients to the
   side of the wok and add noodles.
7. Mix everything together well; add seasoning sauce and continue stir frying
   to mix completely.
8. Add sliced green onion; stir fry quickly and remove from heat.
9. Arrange green lettuce leaves on a plate. Top with the chicken-noodle
   mixture and then a sprinkling of white pepper powder. Serve Immediately.

Kao Soi - Egg Noodles with Chicken in Red Curry Sauce

Ingredients: Step 1 chicken curry

3 tablespoons diced ginger root
2 tablespoons red curry paste
2 tablespoons vegetable oil
2 chicken breasts, cut into small bite-sized
   pieces
1 tablespoon curry powder
1 can (13.5 oz) coconut milk

Seasoning sauce: Step 1 chicken curry

2 tablespoons fish sauce
2 tablespoons palm sugar

Ingredients: Step 2 for side serving

1/4 cup diced shallot
10.5 oz pickled mustard
3 cups water
1 tablespoon white vinegar
14 oz egg (yellow) noodles (fresh or dried)
2 tablespoons vegetable oil
1/2 cup oil for deep-frying
2 tablespoons chopped cilantro
Slices of lime
Chili oil (optional)

Directions: Step 1 chicken curry

1. Peel and dice the ginger; pound well in a mortar.
   Add red curry paste and pound both until well combined.
2. In a small bowl, combine seasoning sauce ingredients and set aside.
3. Heat oil in a pot on medium heat. When oil is hot,
   add curry paste and stir until fragrant.
4. Add cut chicken, stirring until it is partially cooked.
5. Add curry powder and stir thoroughly.
6. Add coconut milk, about 1/2 cup at a time, stirring constantly until chicken
   is cooked through and 1 1/2 cup coconut milk has been added. Reserve
   any remaining coconut milk in the can.
7. Let the mixture simmer about 10 minutes and then add seasoning sauce.
   Bring the mixture to a boil and remove from heat.

Directions: Step 2 for side serving

1. Set aside the diced shallot. Rinse and coarsely chop the pickled mustard.
2. Bring 3 cups of water to a boil. Add chopped mustard and boil for 10
   minutes. Drain; rinse in cold water; and place in a bowl. Add white vinegar
   and mix thoroughly. Set Aside.
3. Separate the noodles loosely. Add them to a pot of enough boiling water
   to cover them. Cook completely; then drain and rinse in cold water.
   Mix in vegetable oil to prevent sticking.
4. Heat 1/2 cup oil in a wok on medium-high heat. When oil is hot, add about
   a handful of cooked noodles and deep-fry until golden brown and crispy.
   Remove from oil and drain on paper towels.
5. Put cooked egg noodles into a bowl; pour chicken-curry sauce over them.
   Add sliced pickled mustard, and diced shallots. Top with crispy noodles,
   chopped cilantro, and 1 tablespoon of remaining coconut milk.
   Serve hot with a slice of lime and chili oil.

Dessert & Beverages

Ingredients:

6 bananas, not too ripe

3/4 cup coconut milk

3/4 cup water

1/3 cup sugar

1 cup coconut milk

3/4 teaspoon salt

1 teaspoon roasted sesame seeds,
   slightly pounded

Directions:

1. Place unpeeled bananas in a pot. Add water to cover them. Place lid on the pot and bring it to a boil. Reduce heat to simmer for about 20 minutes and then drain.
2. Peel and cut each banana in half from top to bottom (like a banana split) and then cut each half into 3 sections.
3. In a pot, mix 3/4 cup of coconut milk and 3/4 cup of water. Simmer until it boils. Add bananas and wait another 10 minutes to add sugar. Cook until soft but not mushy.
4. Add 1 cup of coconut milk and salt. Wait until it boils one more time and turn heat off.
5. Serve warm and topped with roasted sesame seeds.

Bua Loi - Sticky Rice Ball with Taro in Coconut Milk

Ingredients:

1/4 cup glutinous rice flour
1 tablespoon tapioca flour
3 tablespoons water
2 drops purple food color
  (or combining blue and red food color)
2 tablespoons cooked taro
15 cups water (for boiling)
1/4 cup coconut milk
1/4 cup of water
1/4 cup sugar
2 cooked taro, cut in long pieces
1/2 cup coconut milk
1/2 teaspoon salt

Ingredients: for coconut topping

1/4 cup coconut milk
A pinch of salt

Directions:

1. In a mixing bowl, mix the glutinous rice flour, tapioca flour, water, food color, and 2 tablespoons of cooked taro to make a stiff dough.
   If it's too dry, add more water until it's soft enough to hold together.
   Knead well.
2. If the dough is too sticky, coat your hands with tapioca flour before rolling balls. Roll the dough into small balls (about 1/2" diameter).
3. In a medium saucepan, bring 15 cups of water to a boil. Toss in half of the flour balls and boil until cooked (they will float to the surface).
4. Remove with a slotted spoon and put in a bowl of cool water.
   Then repeat with the remaining flour balls. Set them aside and drain when you're ready to add them to the coconut milk in # 5.
5. In a medium pot, mix 1/4 cup of coconut milk, 1/4 cup of water, and sugar. Add the cooked taro pieces. Bring to a boil and add the cooked flour balls.
6. When the mixture returns to a boil again, add 1/2 cup coconut milk and salt. Remove from heat.
7. For the topping: in a small saucepan, combine 1/4 cup coconut milk with salt. Heat just till dissolved; then set aside.
8. Serve warm in individual bowls, each topped with salted coconut milk.

Tab Tim Krobb - Water Chestnut in Coconut Milk Dessert

Ingredients I:

1 cup water chestnuts
1/2 cup water + 1/2 teaspoon red food
    coloring
1 cup tapioca flour
1/4 cup Tao Yai Mom flour (Arrow root flour)
15 cups water (for boiling)

Ingredients II: syrup

1 cup sugar
1 cup water
1/4 teaspoon jasmine essence (optional)

Ingredients III: coconut milk for topping

1 cup coconut milk
1/2 teaspoon salt

Directions:

1. Dice the water chestnuts into 1/8 inch pieces (smaller the better since they will float when in boiling liquid later). Soak them in the diluted red food coloring about 30 minutes until bright red, stirring occasionally. Drain them.
2. Mix 2 flours in a plate. Coat the drained chestnuts with flour and set aside for 10-15 minutes. Then shake chestnuts in the combined flours till well coated.
3. Heat 15 cups of water to a boil. Cook a few water chestnuts at a time, being careful not to overcrowd them, by dropping them into the boiling water. Keep stirring well to avoid them sticking together.
4. When cooked through, they will float on top and look like rubies. Using a slotted spoon or strainer, remove them and plunge into cold water immediately.
5. To make syrup, boil sugar, water, and jasmine essence. Turn the heat off and set it aside to cool.
6. In a saucepan, add coconut milk and salt. Stir until salt dissolves and set it aside to cool.
7. Serve a few water chestnuts in each dessert dish, topped with syrup, salted coconut milk, and crushed ice.

Sa Koo Kao Pod - Tapioca and Corn Pudding with Coconut Milk

Ingredients:

1 3/4 cups water

1/2 cup small Asian-Style tapioca pearls

1/4 teaspoon salt

1/4 cup + 1 tablespoon sugar

3/4 cup corn kernels
   (fresh, frozen or canned)

1/2 cup shredded coconut meat (optional)

1/4 cup coconut milk

Directions:

1. Place the water in a pan and bring to a boil. Add the tapioca pearls and salt. Stir as the water comes back to a boil to avoid it sticking together.

2. Lower the heat slightly to maintain a low boil and cook, stirring frequently to prevent sticking, until the tapioca is completely cooked and soft, 15-20 minutes. When it's cooked, it will look clear (transparent) on the outside but the center still has a small white spot. Just taste some and it shouldn't be hard and crunchy in the center.

3. Stir in sugar until the sugar is thoroughly dissolved. Then stir in the corn kernels and shredded coconut meat. Simmer over low heat for 5 minutes. The kernels should still have a slight fresh crunch.

4. Serve the pudding warm in small bowls, each topped with 1 tablespoon of coconut milk.

Ingredients:

1/2 cup uncooked black sticky rice
1/2 cup uncooked white sticky rice
1 1/2 cups water
1/2 cup water
1 teaspoon tapioca flour*
1 teaspoon water
3 tablespoons sugar
1/2 teaspoon salt
1 cup fruit of your choice
   (fresh, frozen or canned)
* You can substitute tapioca flour with
corn flour or quick-mixing thickening flour.

Ingredients: Coconut topping

1/4 cup coconut milk
1/4 teaspoon salt

Garnish (optional):

Fresh mint leaves

Directions:

1. Mix black and white sticky rice together in a bowl. Rinse and drain twice. Then soak overnight. (Black sticky rice has a thicker grain and requires longer soaking.) When you are ready to use the rice, drain, then rinse and drain one last time.
2. Transfer rice to a microwavable glass bowl. Add just enough warm water to cover the rice.
3. Cover the bowl with its lid and microwave for 5 minutes.
4. Remove from microwave. Stir well and check for doneness. If it is too dry or hard, add a little water, being careful not to add too much. Then microwave for another 5 minutes. Take it out and stir.
5. If the rice is finished cooking, continue with Step 6. If not, repeat the process of adding a little water, microwaving, and stirring except microwave in 1 minute intervals, until the rice is cooked. If it becomes too wet, follow the same 1-minute interval microwaving process until it's perfectly cooked.
6. Place the cooked sticky rice in a pot (or a brass wok). Add 1 1/2 cups water and bring to a boil.
7. Cook rice at medium-low heat for 10 minutes (or a little longer if you prefer extra-soft rice). Stir to prevent sticking. Add an additional 1/2 cup of water; stir well. Continue cooking for another 5 minutes.
8. While the rice cooks, prepare the coconut topping. Mix coconut milk with salt; microwave and stir to dissolve salt. Set it aside.
9. Mix tapioca flour with 1 teaspoon water, stirring to make a paste.
10. When rice has finished cooking, add the tapioca paste and quickly stir. Remove from heat.
11. Add 3 tablespoons sugar (more if you prefer) and salt. Stir to blend well.
12. Spoon hot rice into bowls and then coconut topping over the rice, just enough to cover it. Let individuals mix rice and topping as they like.
13. Garnish with a sprig of fresh mint (optional). Serve along with strawberries, raspberries or canned mixed fruit.

Mun Tom Khing - Sweet Potato in Ginger Syrup

Directions:

1. Peel sweet potatoes, rinse, and cut into 1" thick pieces.
2. Peel ginger root, rinse and thinly slice into pieces.
3. In a pot, on medium-high heat, bring the water to a boil; add ginger, sugar, and salt.
4. When the sugar is dissolved, add the sweet potatoes, continue boiling until the sweet potatoes are cooked and tender.
5. Spoon sweet potatoes, with some of its liquid, into a bowl and serve immediately.

Ingredients:

2 small sweet potatoes
1 small ginger root
3 cups water
1/2 cup sugar
1/4 teaspoon salt

Directions:

1. In a large pot, gently boil 8 cups of water. Drop in a tea bag filled with ice tea mix, leaving the handle of the bag hang outside the pot for easy removal later.
2. Continue boiling for 30 minutes, over medium heat. Remove tea bag and add enough water to the pot to make 8 cups of liquid. Cool; then pour into a pitcher. If desired, you can refrigerate it for a few days.
3. For each serving, pour 1 cup of tea into a glass; mix in 1 tablespoon sweet condensed milk and 1 tablespoon sugar. Add crushed ice and top with 2 tablespoons evaporated milk.

Ingredients: Tea Brew

8 cups water
1 1/2 cups Thai ice tea mix

Ingredients: 1 cup of tea drink

1 cup brewed tea
1 tablespoon sweet condensed milk
1 tablespoon sugar
2 tablespoons evaporated milk

Nam Ta Krai - Lemongrass Drink

Directions:

1. Wash and clean lemongrass. Cut into 3" lengths. Smash lightly just to break apart.
2. Using a pan, roast and stir the lemongrass until an aroma is released and the stalks turn completely brown but not burn.
3. Add roasted lemongrass and Pandan leaf strips to a pot of 4 cups of water and boil about 30 minutes.
4. Add sugar and stir until dissolved.
5. Use cheesecloth to strain the liquid. Serve either hot or cold over crushed ice.

Ingredients:

3 lemongrass stalks
1/4 cup Pandan leaf (optional),
   cut into 1" lengths
4 cups water
3/4 cup sugar
Crushed ice (optional)

Directions:

1. In a large pot, gently boil 8 cups of water. Drop in a tea bag filled with ice tea mix, leaving the handle of the bag hang outside the pot for easy removal later.
2. Continue boiling for 30 minutes, over medium heat. Remove tea bag and add enough water to the pot to make 8 cups of liquid. Cool; then pour into a pitcher. If desired, you can refrigerate it for a few days.
3. For syrup, combine sugar and water in a small saucepan. Bring to a boil and stir until sugar is dissolved. Cool and place in a separate sealed container. Refrigerate.
4. For each serving, pour 1 cup of brewed tea into a glass. Stir in 2 tablespoons syrup (more if you prefer sweeter taste). Squeeze half of a fresh lime and mix well into the tea. Drink with or without ice.

Ingredients: Tea Brew
8 cups water
1 1/2 cups Thai ice tea mix
Fresh limes

Ingredients: Syrup
3/4 cup sugar
2 cups water

Rice & Sticky Rice

Jasmine Rice

Ingredients:
1 1/2 cups Jasmine rice
1 3/4 cups water

Directions: Jasmine rice

1. Rinse the rice twice, moving your fingers through the rice, until the last rinse is clear.
2. Place rice and water in a pot. If you prefer not to measure, add enough water to cover the rice by 3/4 inch.
3. Bring the rice to a boil, covered. Stir it a couple of times to prevent it sticking to the bottom of the pot.
4. Turn the heat down to the lowest setting. Cover and simmer until the rice is cooked through (about 20 minutes). Stir it a couple of times to prevent it sticking to the bottom of the pot.
5. Remove the rice from the heat and allow to sit, still covered, for at least 15 minutes.
6. Fluff with chopsticks or a fork before serving.

Tips: Jasmine rice

1. The amount of water to add can vary depending on the rice.
   New crop rice – rice grown in the same year – is not as dry and needs less water.
2. Cooking jasmine rice in a rice cooker can be tricky.
   Try reducing the amount of water called for in the rice cooker's directions - even to a 1:1 ratio if necessary.
3. 1 1/2 cups jasmine rice gives about 3 1/2 cups cooked rice.
4. Cold jasmine rice is very good for making fried rice.

Sticky Rice

Ingredients:

Sweet rice (or known as sticky rice)

Directions: Sticky rice

1. Place sticky rice in a microwavable glass bowl. Cover with warm water and soak for at least 30 minutes.
2. Rinse rice 2-3 times, until the last rinse is clear.
3. Add just enough warm water to cover the rice. Don't add too much water since rice will be too wet.
4. Cover the bowl with its lid and microwave for 5 minutes.
5. Remove from microwave and stir well. If rice is too dry, add a little water, careful not to add too much.
6. Microwave another 5 minutes; then take it out and stir again.
7. Repeat microwaving and stirring at 1 minute intervals, as long as the rice is too wet, until it's perfectly cooked and soft.

21651245R00043

Made in the USA
San Bernardino, CA
31 May 2015